The Magic of MALAYSIA

CONTENTS

The Land Where the Winds Meet

Situated at the southern extremity of mainland Asia, the Malay Peninsula is strategically placed at the nexus of the seasonal monsoons and straddles one of the world's most ancient and important trade routes; mariners from India, Arabia, the Spice Islands, and the four corners of the Orient named it 'The Land Where the Winds Meet'. Because of its unique location, the Malay Peninsula has always been influenced by outside changes and these have been absorbed into the nation's fabric, creating a multicultural blend of tradition and progress.

Comprising both the Malay Peninsula and the states of Sabah and Sarawak, on the island of Borneo 600km (373 miles) to the east across the South China Sea, Malaysia lies at the heart of Southeast Asia – surrounded by Thailand, the Philippines, Singapore and Indonesia.

Top: *Loaf-shaped Pulau Rengis, a tiny isle offshore from Pulau Tioman, is a popular attraction for snorkellers and scuba divers.*

Above: *Forested limestone hills are characteristic of Perlis, the pocket-sized state in the Peninsula's far northwest.*

From rice paddies to rainforests, tea plantations to palm-oil and rubber estates, Malaysia is overwhelmingly green. Located a few degrees north of the equator, the constant high temperatures, saturating humidity, and frequent rainfall ensure a verdant landscape. The climate varies little throughout the year, apart from the seasonal shift between the northeast and southwest monsoons.

Mangrove-forested wetlands prevail on the Peninsula's west coast and much of the coastline of Sabah and Sarawak, while the east coast is renowned for its long sandy beaches and offshore islands such as Pulau Tioman, which boasts crystal-clear waters and virgin rainforest. Only a century ago vast rainforests stretched from coast to coast, but today most of the Peninsula's lowlands, except for the fertile rice-growing regions in Kedah, Perlis and Kelantan, have been converted to rubber and palm-oil estates, and the forests are now confined to the mountainous interior. Highland tea plantations and temperate vegetable farms thrive on the western watershed of the granite Banjaran Titiwangsa, the mountain range which runs like a spine down the Peninsula from the Thai border. Another sandstone range, the Banjaran Timur, envelops much of the east coast interior and contains Taman Negara, Malaysia's national park, safeguarding a wealth of plant and animal species, and Gunung Tahan, the Peninsula's highest peak. Originating in these rugged highlands are the rivers that not only engendered the establishment of the early sultanates that are today's political states, but also gave them their titles, including the 475km-long (295-mile) Pahang River, which is the longest on the Malaysian mainland.

The Malaysian Peninsula's statistics pall, however, when compared with the geographic splendours of the Bornean states of Sabah and Sarawak: they boast even vaster rainforests, longer rivers, and the incomparable Mount Kinabalu, Southeast Asia's highest peak and the most popular mountain ascent in Malaysia. With its moss-draped forests perpetually shrouded in cloud, Mount Kinabalu has a cool and bracing climate which enables a wide range of plant species (some of which are found nowhere else in the world) to flourish.

Above: Situated in the northern corner of Sabah, Mount Kinabalu ① is the highest mountain between the Himalayas and New Guinea.

Above: The Peninsula state of Kedah is known as Malaysia's 'rice bowl'. Rural scenes, such as this one, are common.

Right: The forests of Sarawak's remote Gunung Mulu National Park ② are home to a wealth of animal and plant species.

Left: Malaysia boasts over 2000 different orchid species, including this tree orchid.

A Wealth of Flora and Fauna

Malaysia's best known ecosystem, the Dipterocarp lowland rainforest, supports a fascinating array of plants. Because the canopy can easily reach 45m (148ft) high – effectively blocking the sunlight from reaching the ground – most plants, including a wealth of orchids, ferns and other epiphytes, grow on the lofty branches and are only visible from the air. Carnivorous pitcher plants grow in montane forest as do rhododendrons (35 species are unique to Sabah). A species of the *Rafflesia*, which is the world's largest flowering plant, is also found in Sabah. Malaysian gardens are characterized by their colourful shrubs, including the hibiscus, which is the nation's national flower, riotous bougainvilleas, and tropical flowering trees such as rain and flame-of-the-forest trees.

Above: The hibiscus, with its vivid blooms, is Malaysia's national flower, and can be seen in gardens all over Malaysia.

The dense rainforest is home to an astounding collection of creatures, including over 200 different mammal species, 722 species of bird, about 1000 varieties of butterflies, and a staggering 8000 different moths; there are insects so numerous that not even experts dare wager a guess. The Malaysian rainforests are among the world's most treasured and at the same time most endangered ecosystems. Large-scale clearing for plantations is now restricted but logging still continues, disturbing animal habitats and opening the country to poachers seeking rhino horn and other rare animal ingredients for Chinese apothecaries. The larger animals, such as the Sumatran rhino, seladang (wild ox) and tiger, are difficult to spot as they are expertly camouflaged in the dense forests. Although the whooping of gibbons is a

Left: A species of the world's largest flower, the Rafflesia, *grows in the forests of Mount Kinabalu Park.*

Right: Pitcher plants obtain their nourishment from insects which fall into their pitchers and dissolve in the sticky fluid.

Above: *The honey bear, also known as the sun bear, is Malaysia's principal omnivore. It seldom attains a height of more than 1.5m (5ft), but is feared by larger animals such as the tiger because of its irritable and unpredictable temper.*

Above: *The yellow-masked angelfish is commonly seen browsing on the extensive coral reefs of eastern Sabah.*

Right: *Wetland forests in the Kuala Selangor Nature Park ③ are home to silvered leaf monkeys, a species of leaf monkey or langur which feeds entirely on leaves.*

familiar sound in the hills, these small apes are rarely seen. Bird-watching, however, is always rewarding. A wide variety of birds can be seen: hornbills with enormous head casques glide above the forest canopy, brilliantly feathered sunbirds and flower-peckers feed amongst the foliage, while pheasants, jungle fowl and pittas peck about on the forest floor.

In the mangrove and nipah-palm forests of Malaysia's wetlands are bizarre fish like the mudskipper which walks about on crutch-like fins, the archer fish which shoots its prey with a jet of water, as well as estuarine crocodiles which are most prevalent in Sarawak. Extensive coral reefs support a wide variety of corals and abundant fish life in the oceans surrounding the offshore islands of both mainland and Bornean Malaysia, and turtles, including the giant leatherback, make their annual nesting migrations to palm-fringed beaches on the Peninsula's east coast and the offshore islands of Sabah.

Above: *The atlas moth (Attacus atlas), has a wing span of 25cm (10in), and is the largest of the more than 8000 different moth species found in Malaysia.*

From Trading Kingdoms to Independence

So much has been written about Melaka, capital of the powerful trading kingdom of the same name which introduced Islam and provided a template for Malay traditions in stagecraft, social behaviour and culture, that it is assumed that Malaysia's historical era began with the founding of this legendary port in the late 14th century. Although there is no denying that Melaka was the greatest of all Malay trading nations, there were others which preceded it, such as sixth-century Langkasuka (famed for its camphor wood), seventh-century Chih Tu whose monarch had an ocean-going fleet for transporting rainforest exports, and Kedah Tua (Old Kedah) which ruled the northwest from the fifth to the 14th century. Kedah Tua is the only kingdom to precede Melaka which has confirmed its location with Buddhist and Hindu temple remains.

In 1511, the Melakan Sultanate was overthrown by the Portuguese. In the euphoria of conquest, the Portuguese aimed to control the spice trade as their Melakan predecessors had, but when the all-powerful Muslim traders defected to Islamic Sumatran ports and the ousted sultanate continually waged war from its new base in Johor, Portuguese coffers were diminished and the world's 'richest sea port' never attained its former glory – neither under this colonial power nor under the Dutch who took it in 1641 nor the English who claimed it in 1795.

Meanwhile, other peninsular sultanates rose to power, notably Johor (run by the Melaka heirs) which counted Selangor, Pahang and Terengganu amongst its vassals in the 17th century. Although the sultanates were not dominated by the colonial powers, they could not exert enough influence to dominate other states as the Melakan sultanate had done before the coming of the Europeans.

In 1786 the Sultan of Kedah was persuaded to cede Penang to the British, and in 1819 Singapore was established, effectively ending the Malay grip on the trading world. The Straits Settlements, comprising Penang, Province Wellesley (the opposite mainland province), Melaka and Singapore, were ceded to the British in 1826, and gradually English intervention spread into the interior with Perak, Selangor, Negeri Sembilan and Pahang becoming a protectorate in 1896. Kedah, Perlis, Kelantan and Terengganu (previously under the control of the Thais) accepted British residents in 1909 although their rulers still exercised more independence than did the sultans of the protectorate. By 1919 the

6

Above: *The Porta de Santiago in Melaka is the last surviving remnant of the Portuguese fort of A Famosa, which was built in the early 16th century.*

Union Jack flew over the entire Peninsula, while across the South China Sea, Sarawak was under the dominion of the Brooke dynasty, the self-styled 'White Rajahs' who began their rule when James Brooke, an adventurous Englishman, assisted the Sultan of Brunei during a rebellion and was rewarded with the gift of a large chunk of Borneo as his personal fief. Meanwhile, Sabah was under the control of the British North Borneo Company, and all the lands now currently embraced by Malaysia were in English hands until the Japanese Occupation during World War II.

After the war ended in 1945, the Malays agitated for independence and on 15 August 1957, Britain finally relinquished its sovereignty, and the first prime minister, Tunku Abdul Rahman, declared Malaya independent. In 1963, Singapore, Sabah and Sarawak joined Malaya to form Malaysia; however, only two years later, Singapore became a separate republic. Today, Malaysia has developed into one of the strongest economies in Southeast Asia with an on-target prediction of attaining the status of a developed nation by the year 2020.

Right: *Young Sabahans celebrate Independence Day, 31 August, in Kota Kinabalu.*

Government and Economy

Malaysia is a parliamentary democracy with a prime minister as head of state. Each of the 13 states has its own state government, headed by a chief minister. Nine of the states still retain a sultan or rajah, who acts as the custodian of Malay culture and religion for his state. In addition, the constitution also provides for the appointment of a paramount ruler. One of the heads of state is elected as the paramount ruler, or king (a ceremonial position), on a rotating basis every five years.

Malaysia's economy today has been considerably influenced by its early years of British rule. In the latter years of the 19th century, Malaya was the jewel in the British Empire, boosting its coffers with tin and rubber profits. Employing a 'divide and rule' strategy, the British rulers ensured that Chinese immigrants who had initially been imported to work the tin mines were encouraged to stay in commerce while the Malays were trained for government. This imbalance effectively put the control of the economy in Chinese hands, but communal troubles in the 1960s led to the introduction of a series of economic policies to improve the position of the Malays and to erase the colonial stamp of identifying races by their occupation and material status.

Below: Flying the Malaysian flag, the world's tallest flagpole towers over Kuala Lumpur's 19th-century Jame Mosque.

Rubber, the boom crop synonymous with Malaya, took over from tin as the major economic contributor in 1913 and stayed in the lead until 1980 when it was overtaken by palm oil. Vast plantations of both of these crops cover the lowlands of most states. In the last decade, manufacturing has been making inroads into the economy.

Malaysia's 'Look East' policy, initiated in the 1980s by the country's fourth prime minister Datuk Seri Dr Mahathir Mohamad, found new Asian sources of support and development, and a highly successful policy of heavy industrialization including the production of a national car and the development of oil and natural gas refineries (today, both significant earners of foreign currency) was launched.

Malaysia's natural heritage, combined with such fascinating ethnic diversity, is the major reason why tourism is such a money-spinner for the nation. Sun-lovers are attracted by the white palm-fringed sands of tropical islands such as Pangkor, Langkawi, Perhentian and Tioman; history buffs are lured by Melaka's rich and fascinating heritage; food-lovers flock to Penang

Above: A tourist launches into the air to parasail above the ocean off Batu Feringghi, a popular beach on the resort island of Penang. ④

Right: Fishermen still draw in their catch by hand at Pantai Sri Tujuh in Kelantan's far north.

for its renowned cuisine; shoppers are drawn to Kuala Lumpur's vibrant markets and sophisticated shopping malls; adventurers head for Taman Negara's pristine rainforests and the mountains of Sabah, and embark on adventurous upriver safaris in Sarawak; scuba divers descend on the oceanic island of Sipadan, situated off the east coast of Sabah, for world-class diving in clear waters; and travellers fascinated by the nation's cultural spectrum can time their visit to coincide with annual events such as the giant kite festival, held in the Malay state of Kelantan on the Peninsula's east coast, or the lion dances and other colourful processions that are a feature of the Chinese New Year.

Above: Tea bushes carpet the hills at Boh Tea's Sungai Palas Estate in the Cameron Highlands,⑤ which produces Malaysia's best teas.

Above: These oil palms, planted with ground cover which prevents soil erosion, will only bear oil-producing seed kernels after three years.

9

The People of Malaysia

As Malaysia's name suggests, the Malays are the dominant ethnic group in the country, numbering over half of the population of almost 18 million, while those of Chinese ancestry account for one-third, and those of Indian descent about one-tenth. The remainder comprises a remarkable diversity of indigenous peoples, including the Peninsula's Orang Asli (original people), the nomadic Penan of Sarawak, the Iban – once renowned as the headhunters of Borneo – the Kayan-Kenyah people of upriver Sarawak, the Kelabit of Sarawak's Central Highlands, the Kadazan from around Mount Kinabalu, the Bajau from Sabah's coast, the crosscultural Baba Nonya from Melaka, and the Portuguese Eurasians who descended from Melaka's Portuguese conquerors of the 16th century.

Below: A becak, *or trishaw, driver awaits customers in Penang's capital, Georgetown, where this mode of transport is still a popular way of exploring the city.*

Bahasa Malaysia is the official language of all Malaysians (although English, Tamil and Chinese dialects are widely spoken) and its mixture of Arabic, Sanskrit, Hindi, Turkish, Persian, and Javanese words, to name only a few, is indicative of the mixture of cultural traditions in Malaysia, known as *adat*, which are separate from religion.

Malaysia's oldest inhabitants are the Orang Asli known as Semang, or Negritos, who formerly lived a nomadic existence in the vast northern rainforests of Peninsular Malaysia but who now are semi-settled at the forest fringes. Other Orang Asli groups include the 40,000-strong Senoi, who are masters of the blowpipe, and the Mah Meri and Jah Hut, who are excellent wood-carvers.

Among the indigenous peoples of Sabah are the prosperous rice-growing Kadazan; the coastal Malays, the Bajaus, renowned for their nautical skills and horsemanship; the Illanun, once the region's fiercest pirates; the Suluk, of the original sultanate; and the agile Idahan who collect edible birds' nests from cave ceilings, which are exported to China.

Sarawak's oldest inhabitants are the coastal Melanau of the peat swamps who lived a semi-aquatic existence; the Iban, the largest ethnic group, some of whom still live in longhouses; the peaceful Bidayuh; the upriver Kayan and Kenyah renowned

Above: *Sarawak's older Kayan women still use heavy brass rings to elongate their ear lobes – an ancient decorative practice of this tribe.*

Above: Wearing the typical Johorean attire of collarless shirt and black velvet songkok, this Malay man enters a mosque in the town of Batu Pahat.

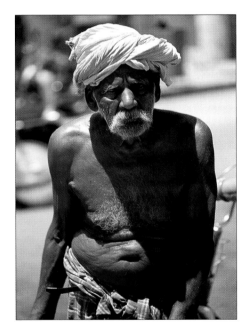

for their navigational skills and dance; the highland Kelabit famed for their rice-growing; the Muruts who still practise shifting agriculture; and the nomadic Penan, whose lifestyles are the most endangered and whose ideas on sustainable land use are ironically the most up to date.

Chinese and Indian traders have been coming to Malaysia for over a thousand years. Initially, the communities were small, such as the Baba Nonya people of Melaka whose Chinese ancestors intermarried with Malays. There were enormous demographic changes during the 19th and 20th centuries when the British administration encouraged large-scale immigrations for labour on the rubber estates and tin mines. Teochew, Cantonese, Hokkien, and Hakka peoples immigrated initially to work the tin mines, bringing their religion, culture, dialects, and their co-operative societies which later formed the basis of their economic success. All Malaysian cities and towns have a Chinatown, characterized by shophouses, temples and the ubiquitous corner coffee shop.

The largest Indian population, of Tamil descent, is found on the mainland. Although they still make up the majority of the rubber-estate labour, Indians are found in all walks of life and Hindu temples are a common sight in Peninsula towns. Muslim Indian traders were amongst the earliest and most influential visitors to Malaysia's shores and successfully integrated into the Malay way of life. Known as *mamak*, the offspring of Indian Muslim and Malay parentage are a well-known part of Penang society; the prime minister, Datuk Seri Dr Mahathir Mohamad, is of this parental background.

Below: An elaborate headdress is part of the traditional ceremonial dress of the Bajau people of Sabah, also known as the 'Sea Gypsies'.

Left: A Malay schoolgirl participates in the Merdeka Day parade in Kuala Lumpur.

Religion and Culture

In Penang there is a street which aptly reflects the diversity of Malaysia's multi-ethnic and multi-religious population. Its old name is Pitt Street but it is now called Jalan Masjid Kapitan Keling, after the mosque of the same name built by Indian Muslims from British India who accompanied Francis Light, the city's founder, to the area in the late 18th century. Situated one block north is the Mahamariamman Temple, Penang's oldest Hindu place of worship, another two blocks further is the Goddess of Mercy Temple, the island's most popular Chinese shrine, while at the head of the street is St George's Anglican Church, one of the oldest churches in Southeast Asia. Embracing the four great religions of the world, the street is evidence of the nation's remarkable ethnic harmony. Malaysia's rich cultural fabric is the product of centuries of trade, immigration, shifting settlements, and colonialism – all as a result of its key geographical position.

Islam, the Malay religion, dominates in Malaysia. To be Malay is to be Muslim. Islam is the governing force in a Muslim's life, beginning at birth when the declaration of faith is whispered in a baby's ear. Nationwide, the call to prayer five times a day is amplified from the minarets of contemporary mosques in the cities, and pounded by a drum roll in the villages. The protocol of Malay courts, including the rituals and regalia, originated in Indian Muslim states, as did the Malay wedding ceremony.

Besides Islam, virtually all of the world's major religions are represented in Malaysia, including Buddhism, Hinduism and Christianity. Buddhism, which was introduced by Chinese immigrants in the 15th century, is the second largest religion in Malaysia after Islam. Some influences, however, are even older, like the traditional medicine men, or *bomoh*, whose chants are derived from ancient animist beliefs. Many of the isolated

12

indigenous peoples in Malaysia still profess the animism of their ancestors. Their belief was that everything, both animate and inanimate, contained a soul, including the skulls of their enemies.

Malaysia has an intriguing cultural heritage, enriched by the traditional festivals of the Malays, Chinese and Indians, as well as the numerous ethnic tribes of Sabah and Sarawak. Islamic holidays, such as the fasting month of Ramadan and the festivities at its close, are the most important yearly events in the Malay calendar. Chinese festivities complete with traditional opera are among the noisiest and most colourful on Malaysia's jam-packed calendar of cultural events. The Indian communities of the Peninsula are well known for their sacred temple dances, which are also performed at cultural events, and their vibrant festivals and processions including the pilgrimage to Kuala Lumpur's Batu Caves during Thaipusam when thousands of devotees pierce their bodies as an act of penitence. Harvest festivals are held by both the Kadazan in Sabah and Sarawak's Iban tribe. These thanksgiving celebrations are characterized by the consumption of rice wine, and much feasting and dancing. In the longhouses of Sarawak, traditional dances, such as the famous Hornbill Dance, are still performed.

Most of the Malay arts and crafts like batik, silk-weaving, silverware, and wood-carving are produced in the east coast states of Peninsular Malaysia. Kelantan is the centre of traditional pastimes such as kite flying, top spinning, shadow-puppet performances, and *rebana* drum contests. Of all the traditional artefacts produced in Sabah and Sarawak, the Iban *pua kumbu* (an intricately woven ceremonial hanging) is the most interesting. Designs, which are passed down from one generation to the next, may feature stylized birds, animals or plants, or motifs representing mythical subjects that have special spiritual significance.

AROUND THE CAPITAL

Kuala Lumpur, Malaysia's capital, the youngest of Southeast Asia's booming national hubs, is a city in a hurry. Skylines change by the day, cranes hover over city blocks and construction workers toil around the clock to complete projects including a rapid-transit rail system and the 88-storey twin towers of Kuala Lumpur City Centre which, when completed, will be one of the world's tallest edifices. Built as a mining settlement only 150 years ago on the banks of the muddy estuary that gave the city its name, KL, as it is known, is the largest city in Malaysia.

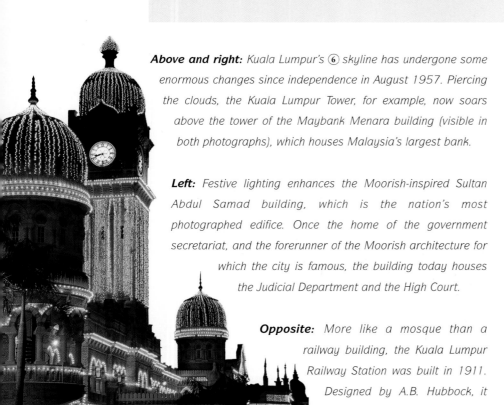

Above and right: *Kuala Lumpur's ⑥ skyline has undergone some enormous changes since independence in August 1957. Piercing the clouds, the Kuala Lumpur Tower, for example, now soars above the tower of the Maybank Menara building (visible in both photographs), which houses Malaysia's largest bank.*

Left: *Festive lighting enhances the Moorish-inspired Sultan Abdul Samad building, which is the nation's most photographed edifice. Once the home of the government secretariat, and the forerunner of the Moorish architecture for which the city is famous, the building today houses the Judicial Department and the High Court.*

Opposite: *More like a mosque than a railway building, the Kuala Lumpur Railway Station was built in 1911. Designed by A.B. Hubbock, it features domes and minarets.*

16

Above: A devotee kneels in prayer before a Buddhist shrine decorated in Thai style.

Below: At an Indian temple in Kuala Lumpur, fresh banana leaves decorate the doorway and a fire burns outside; these are both symbols of Hinduism, the predominant faith of Malaysia's inhabitants of Indian descent who number around 10 percent of the total Peninsular population.

Opposite and above: Located at the confluence of the Klang and Gombak rivers, on the site where Kuala Lumpur was founded, the Masjid Jame, which was built at the turn of the century after the fashion of a North Indian mosque, is a haven of peace and quiet in the centre of the city.

Below: St Mary's Church, overlooking Merdeka Square, was built in 1907 and served as the principal place of worship for English bureaucrats and planters during the colonial era. It was designed by Spooner, a versatile architect influenced by Moorish style.

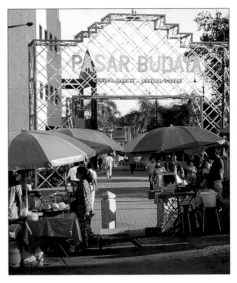

Above: The Pasar Budaya, which literally means 'culture market', is situated in KL's Central Market. Here, craftspeople sell their wares, including batik and silk-weaving.

Above and opposite: Petaling Street, the hub of Kuala Lumpur's Chinatown, is the city's most popular night market. Famed for its pirated wares and bargain-basement shopping, its vendors sell everything from fake designer watches to tropical fruits.

Below: The Pasar Malam, or night market, such as this one in Jalan Tunku Abdul Rahman where a vendor is selling deep-fried snacks, is one of Kuala Lumpur's most popular after-hours local eating areas.

Right: Not the highest, but certainly the most elegant of Kuala Lumpur's skyscrapers, the marble-sided Dayabumi building combines old Moorish style with late-20th-century architecture.

Above and left: *Hindu statues adorn the interior of the Batu Caves art museum located inside the renowned cave system near Kuala Lumpur which is entered by climbing 272 stairs. The Temple Cave, with a 101m-high (330ft) ceiling, contains a century-old shrine devoted to the Hindu god, Lord Subramaniam. During the festival of Thaipusam, which commemorates the deities' victory over evil, vast crowds flock to the caves to witness the pilgrimage of over a thousand devotees bearing sacrificial loads known as kavadis. These wooden frames are decorated with flowers and feathers. Some devotees defy all sense of pain by piercing their cheeks, tongues and chests with metal spikes.*

Opposite: *The highest minarets in the world soar over the computer-designed dome of the Selangor state mosque, known as Masjid Sultan Salahuddin Abdul Aziz, which is located in the state capital, Shah Alam,⑦ on the outskirts of Kuala Lumpur. Twenty thousand worshippers can pray at one time in the great hall which features an enormous chandelier.*

Right: *Thaipusam, a festival celebrated by Hindus of Indian descent, is evident throughout Malaysia, but it is at its most colourful at the Batu Caves ⑧ on the outskirts of Kuala Lumpur in Selangor state.*

MELAKA AND NEGERI SEMBILAN

Melaka, formerly Malacca, the famous trading empire that ruled much of the Malay world during the 15th century, is located on the southwest coast of the Peninsula. The nation's most historical town, Melaka bears witness to its six centuries of existence with ruins and heritage buildings from the Portuguese, Dutch and English colonial eras; it also boasts the best-preserved Chinatown in Southeast Asia. Negeri Sembilan, the neighbouring state, was first settled by the Minangkabau people from Sumatra during the early 15th century.

Top: *A replica of the original Melaka Sultanate Palace was reconstructed in the 1980s from a 15th-century description of Sultan Mansur Shah's palace during Melaka's golden era.*

Below: *The ruins of Porta de Santiago and St Paul's Church are the only tangible remains of the 16th-century Portuguese fortress in Melaka ⑨ known as A Famosa.*

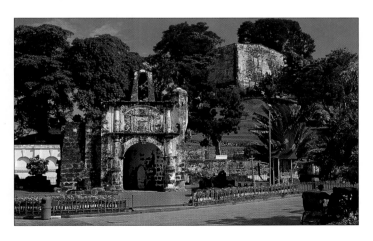

Above: *Within the walls of the remains of St Paul's Church, which was built by the Portuguese in 1521, are massive granite tombstones dating from Dutch times.*

Opposite: *Melaka's historical town square is home to 17th-century Dutch buildings, including the striking Christ Church which still contains its original pews.*

Above: *Fanlights, carved balustrades and stucco decorations adorn this 19th-century townhouse on Jalan Hang Jebat.*

Left: *Two-storey shophouses, with columns covered in Chinese calligraphy, are a common sight in the old shopping district.*

Right: *Trishaws, known as* becak, *are the best way to tour Melaka's famous sights.*

Opposite: *Lined with century-old Chinese shophouses, Jalan Tukang Emas, 'The Goldsmiths' Street', is viewed from the minaret of the historic Kampung Keling Mosque which was built in 1748.*

Above: *This contemporary residence in the royal town of Sri Menanti in Negeri Sembilan is clearly inspired by traditional Minangkabau architecture which originates from Sumatra.*

Below: *The dramatically curved roof ridges on the Taman Seri Budaya cultural centre in Seremban,* ⑩ *the capital of Negeri Sembilan, are designed in the shape of buffalo horns, the symbol of the Minangkabau people.*

Above: *Nestled amongst coconut palms in Sri Menanti, the Istana Besar is home to the current Yang di-Pertuan Besar, the ruler of Negeri Sembilan, whose Sumatran ancestors settled here over four centuries ago.*

Opposite: *The roof of this rural home echoes the distinctive curves of the regional architecture.*

HILL STATIONS

Lured by the cool climate of the highlands and the mountainous interior, the English colonials built hill stations in Malaysia as an escape from the heat of the lowlands, and also as an opportunity to recreate something of their homeland. Tudor-style hotels and retreats with rose gardens are still maintained at Cameron Highlands and Fraser's Hill in Pahang, as well as at Penang Hill and Bukit Larut in Perak. The Cameron Highlands is also the 'tea capital' of Malaysia, and most of the nation's fruit and vegetables are grown here.

Top: Lush montane rainforests swathe the highlands surrounding the old-fashioned mountain resort of Fraser's Hill, ⑪ *a mere two-hour drive from Kuala Lumpur.*

Left: This Temiar, from the lower Perak foothills, lives in a village on the side of the Highlands road.

Above and right: Malaysia's only casino is found at Genting Highlands, ⑫ *the nearest hill resort to Kuala Lumpur. Chinese shrines at the resort are popular with gamblers who pray for good luck.*

Opposite: Mist-shrouded rainforests surround the Cameron Highlands ⑤ *in the far northwest corner of Pahang state.*

30

Opposite and above: *Undulating rows of manicured tea bushes carpet the hills of the Cameron Highlands ⑤ where tea estates began in the 1930s. Besides producing the bulk of the nation's tea crop, the region is also known for its vegetable and flower farms.*

Above: *Chinese Buddhists worship at the Sam Poh Temple at Brinchang,⑭ the highest town in the Cameron Highlands.*

Right: *Montane rainforest surrounds the fairways of the Cameron Highlands golf course where local Orang Asli youths are employed as caddies.*

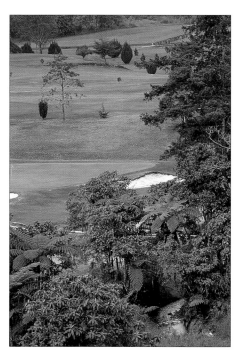

Below: *Overlooking the golf course in Tanah Rata,⑬ Ye Olde Smokehouse has been a hotel since the Highlands' earliest days, and still maintains its colonial atmosphere with carefully preserved Tudor-style buildings, immaculate English cottage gardens, and log fires in the dining room where roast beef dinners are still served.*

Above, below and right: *Terraced vegetable farms are carved from the hills in the Cameron Highlands,⑤ especially in the region north of Brinchang which includes Tringkap, Kuala Terla and Kampung Raja. Temperate vegetables such as cabbages and potatoes thrive here, while strawberry and flower farms are also a major source of the region's wealth. Water is tapped from hill streams and gravity-fed to the market gardens below. Erosion is a problem, however, especially when higher slopes are cleared for farms.*

THE PENINSULA'S NORTHWEST

Along the populous west coast north of Kuala Lumpur is Perak, which is the second-largest Peninsula state, and the heart of the nation's tin-mining region; it also boasts the royal capital of Kuala Kangsar and the resort island of Pulau Pangkor. Further north is Pulau Penang, Malaysia's best-known tourist destination. It is renowned for its beach resorts and vibrant capital, Georgetown, with its historic streetscapes, bazaars and unique cuisine. Neighbouring Penang is Kedah, the nation's 'rice bowl' with its famous resort isles of Langkawi.

Opposite and left: Kellie's Castle near Batu Gajah, south of Ipoh, ⑮ was built by a rich planter, William Kellie Smith, in the 1920s; he died before it was completed.

Top: Work on the Ubudiah Mosque in Kuala Kangsar ⑯ was delayed in 1913 when a shipment of Italian marble was destroyed by a royal elephant who ran amok.

Below: Traditional Malay woodcraft skills, including intricate carvings, are evident at the Royal Museum in Kuala Kangsar which was once the home of the Sultan of Perak.

Following pages: Luxury sea villas at Pulau Pangkor Laut Resort, on the tiny, privately owned island of Pangkor Laut, ⑰ are lapped by the emerald-green waters of Royal Bay.

Above: *Soaring above Georgetown, ⑱ the KOMTAR tower is a prominent landmark in the north of Penang.*

Left: *Georgetown's historic heart is still characterized by quaint red-roofed Chinese shophouses and heritage buildings.*

Below: *Located at the northern end of Batu Feringghi beach, the Rasa Sayang Resort is Penang's ④ most luxurious hotel.*

Below right: *The last of the great colonial-style hotels, the Eastern and Oriental Hotel, better known as the E & O, once hosted Somerset Maugham, the famous English novelist, and actress Rita Hayworth.*

Right: *The funicular railway up Penang Hill descends over a stone viaduct built in 1899. The journey up the hill is still very popular.*

Opposite: *Along Penang's famous Batu Feringghi beach, resorts like the Golden Sands, seen here from an elevated suite, are a year-round holiday destination for both domestic and international tourists.*

Above: *A smiling Buddha is only one of 10,000 images at the Kek Lok Si Temple complex at Air Hitam, the largest Buddhist temple in Malaysia.*

Above right: *Mythical Thai figures guard the entrance to the main hall of the Wat Chayamangkalaram.*

Opposite: *Construction of the Kek Lok Si Temple began in 1899 after a visiting Buddhist abbot envisaged the site as a crane with outstretched wings.*

Right, top and bottom: *Urns full of incense sticks, devotional lamps and prayer sheets within Penang's temples.*

Below: *Elaborately decorated gables are a feature of the 31-room Cheong Fatt Tze Mansion in Georgetown which was built by a Chinese tycoon in 1870.*

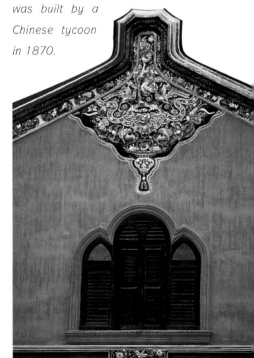

Left: *Deckchairs beckon beachgoers at Pantai Chenang, undoubtedly Pulau Langkawi's ⑲ best-known beach which boasts luxury and moderately priced resorts, well-known restaurants, creamy-white sands, and wonderful sunsets.*

Opposite: *Surrounded by towering coconut palms, this traditional Kedah-style house on Pulau Langkawi features a thatched roof made with the fronds of the nipah, a trunk-less palm. The house is raised on stilts in case of floods, and to allow cooling breezes to circulate beneath the floorboards; it used to ensure safety from marauding tigers.*

Below: *Alor Setar's ⑳ Balai Besar (The Large Audience Hall) dates from 1904 when it was built to stage five royal weddings. The roof style shows Thai influences, derived from a time when Kedah was under Siamese suzerainty.*

Above left and right: *Stunning views of palm-fringed beaches, tranquil waters and offshore islands are some of the many attractions of Pulau Langkawi, the largest of a 104-island archipelago off the far north-west coast of the Peninsula.*

Below: *Alor Setar, the capital of Kedah, has many historic buildings including the majestic Masjid Zahir, a Moorish-style mosque that was built in 1912. It features distinctive black domes in the style of Acehnese architecture from Sumatra.*

Above: *Tiny anchovy-like fish, known as* ikan bilis, *a mainstay of Malay cuisine, are boiled in sea water and then dried on mats in the sun at Empangan Malut, a fishing village on Pulau Langkawi.* ⑲

Above: *A water buffalo grazes on rice stubble, the remains of the harvest which takes place in the dry season around December and January.*

Right: *Villagers still thresh the paddy in the traditional way and rice is still the economic mainstay inland away from the tourist-dominated regions.*

RAINFORESTS

Malaysia's rainforests are among the world's oldest; when the last ice age struck both the Amazon and the Congo regions, Southeast Asia's forests remained undisturbed. Only a century ago, the forests swathed the Peninsula and the island of Borneo, from the east to the west coasts, but logging and plantations have reduced their size considerably. Vast forested regions still remain, however, and many of Malaysia's national parks still contain virgin forests which are home to an enormous range of plantlife and animals.

Left: The mighty Tahan River is studded with rapids between Kuala Tahan and Kuala Trenggan, and provides an exciting river trip by motorized longboat.

Above: Sunlight filters through the canopy of the lowland Dipterocarp forests; trees can attain incredible heights while plantlife is sparse on the dimly lit forest floor.

Opposite: Malaysia's oldest national park, Taman Negara, ㉑ sprawls over the interior of Pahang, Terengganu, and Kelantan, including over 4000km² (1544 sq miles) of virgin rainforest habitat.

Right: Hikers enjoy the view from Bukit Teresek which, on a clear day, extends to the mountains of the Banjaran Timur, including Gunung Tahan.

Left: *Flowering lotuses are a familiar sight in Malaysian waterways, especially at Tasek Chini, a series of lakes in Pahang, where the annual blooming is a colourful event.*

Opposite: *This elevated walkway, strung through the canopy of Taman Negara, is the best way to appreciate the rainforest as some plants and animals are found only in the mid- and upper levels of the forest. The vegetation is so dense that it is often very difficult to see gibbons and other mammals.*

Above: *Coffee is grown on both sides of the South China Sea, in Sabah, Sarawak and Peninsular Malaysia, by small-scale farmers.*

Above: *Taman Negara is home to around 14,500 species of plants and trees, including the night ghost tree with its 'footprint' leaves.*

Above: *Rubber trees are tapped around dawn, and the latex is collected mid-morning; the process has hardly changed over time.*

Left: *Perched at the edge of a mangrove forest in Kuala Selangor Nature Park,③ this hide offers bird-watchers the chance to observe resident and migratory species.*

Opposite: *Rainforest giants overhang the Tahan River, the major tributary flowing through Taman Negara.*

Above and below: *An Orang Asli hunter of the Senoi group brings down a squirrel with his blowpipe while the woman below is from the Endau–Rompin Forest Reserve region.㉒ The Senoi are experts with the blowpipe and their economy still involves the collecting of rainforest products.*

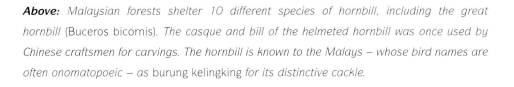

Above: *Malaysian forests shelter 10 different species of hornbill, including the great hornbill (Buceros bicornis). The casque and bill of the helmeted hornbill was once used by Chinese craftsmen for carvings. The hornbill is known to the Malays – whose bird names are often onomatopoeic – as* burung kelingking *for its distinctive cackle.*

THE PENINSULA'S EAST COAST

Pantai Timur, or the east coast, extends the length of the Malay Peninsula, from Kelantan through the states of Terengganu and Pahang to the southern tip of the Johor peninsula. Historically, geographically and culturally distinct from the more populous and multicultural west coast, the east is more Malay dominated and, as a result, many traditional crafts, arts and pastimes still survive. Beautiful beaches are found along this sun-drenched stretch, and the tropical islands with their coconut groves and forested slopes are quite unique.

Above and opposite: Women control the vast fruit and vegetable hall at Kota Bharu's ㉓ Central Market where a wonderful array of local and Thai produce is on sale. The huge beans are from the petai, a lofty rainforest tree, and they are eaten to lower blood pressure. Cabbages, cauliflowers and other vegetables are grown in the Cameron Highlands.

Right: Natural light streams through the dome onto the market floor. The upper floors house cafés and foodstalls, as well as stalls selling an enormous range of products from hand-painted silk batiks to coconut biscuits or quails' eggs.

Left: Hawkers travel around villages and even city suburbs on motorized carts, providing a service for those without transportation to the markets.

Left: *Birds are kept in elaborate split bamboo cages and contests are held on weekends when judges decide which one has the perfect song.*

Opposite: *Batik sarongs are favoured by Malay women; on the east coast, making batik is a vital cottage industry.*

Above and below: *Flying and building extremely large kites is a popular windy season pastime in the state of Kelantan.*

Above: *Hamzah, a master puppeteer from Kelantan, displays some of the dozens of shadow puppets he uses for each show. He* narrates and moves the characters, which are made from leather stretched over a bamboo frame, then painted, and he also conducts the band and performs the necessary 'magic' rituals.

Left and right: *Traditional musical instruments are still popular in Kelantan.*

Above: *At Pantai Sabak on Kelantan's northern coastline, fishing boats may be motorized but they are still painted in traditional stripes with mythological-inspired motifs. The original bird-shaped spar holder is believed to contain the 'soul' or 'spirit' of the boat.*

Left: *This imposing mosque is one of many on the east coast which has a long and famous religious history. Islam first arrived on Malaysian shores at Terengganu in the mid-14th century.*

Opposite and below: *Pulau Perhentian,㉔ Malaysia's most quintessential tropical island, is the largest of a duo of islands in the South China Sea, lying off the northern Terengganu coast. Dazzling white beaches, crystal seas perfect for snorkelling and scuba diving, and very few villages and roads provide travellers with a 'Robinson Crusoe' experience.*

Above: More than 64 islands are scattered off the coast of Johor, ranging from tiny islets, such as this one, to larger well-known resort islands such as Pulau Besar and Pulau Rawa. The surrounding waters of the South China Sea, including the coral reefs, are classified as a marine park to protect these fragile and valuable ecosystems.

Opposite: Juara, a fishing port on the east coast of Pulau Tioman, ㉕ is only accessible by boat or by a mountainous trail through virgin rainforests.

Right: Snowy white beaches, clear azure waters, coconut groves, and tangled rainforests combine to make Pulau Tioman one of the world's most spectacular tropical islands. Located 32km (20 miles) off the coast of Pahang, the island is reached by air from KL or by ferry from Mersing.

SARAWAK

Malay sultanates ruled the Bornean coast, and the Iban, Kayan, Kenyah and other indigenous peoples roamed the interior of what is presently the state of Sarawak before the coming of James Brooke. An adventurous Englishman who helped the Sultan of Brunei suppress an uprising, Brooke was rewarded with this vast state as his personal fief. The 'White Rajahs' controlled Sarawak for a century. Sarawak is one of the world's last untamed wildernesses; it is renowned for its rainforests, mighty rivers and enormous cave complexes.

Above: Crowding the banks of the Sarawak River, Kuching, 26 the state capital, reflects the nation's growing prosperity in its high-rise buildings, and in the recently revamped riverside promenade.

Opposite: The lights of Kuching and a tropical sunset reflect in the languid waters of the Sarawak River, which historians say has been visited by traders since the 10th century AD.

Above and right: At the indoor market on the riverside, a local shows off his produce and a gaping smile.

Left: Kuching's town mosque rises above the traditional shophouses of old Chinatown.

Left: *Wearing original headgear, this Iban shows how to use the blowpipe, although these days the majority of Borneo's largest inland farming group are more at ease hunting with a shotgun than with this traditional weapon.*

Above: *Partially submerged houses, such as this one on the banks of a swollen river in Sarawak, are the result of torrential rains.*

Opposite: *A Sarawak longhouse can hold up to 30 families, each living in individual quarters known as units but sharing a common veranda space where work and social events take place.*

Right: *Iban children play at the river where they learn to swim from an early age. Although many Iban are now Christians, they still revere traditional heroes and deities and some believe in dreams as omens.*

Above right: *Longboats with outboard motors are the most popular method of travel through the river-riddled interior.*

Right: *Stretched ear lobes, a traditional mark of beauty, can still be seen on older Kayan-Kenyah women.*

Opposite: *At the Sarawak Cultural Centre near Kuching,* ㉖ *where regional homes and lifestyles are re-enacted, bamboo is crafted into a bridge in the fashion of the Bidayuh from southern Sarawak.*

Above: *In this longhouse complex, versatile and long-lasting corrugated iron has replaced the traditional thatched roofs.*

Right: *Traditional costumes, such as these boars' teeth breastplates and feathered headdresses, are only worn on ceremonial occasions. Most Sarawakian ethnic groups retain their customs despite modernization.*

Below left: *This old longhouse on the Makabu River contains dozens of families and is a survivor of the days when nearly all inland Sarawak communities lived in dwellings which could reach 300m (984ft) in length. A traditional longhouse was made entirely from natural, homegrown materials, including the wall behind which was constructed from split bamboo matting. Longhouse dwellers sit on woven pandanus mats to weave, dine and socialize.*

Above: *In the higher realms of Mount Mulu, the second-highest peak in Sarawak, pitcher plants grow in abundance.*

Opposite: *Aptly named longboats transport visitors to Gunung Mulu National Park ② in the remote northeast of Sarawak. Encompassing 52,866ha (130,632 acres), the park contains an awesome cave system, including the Deer Cave and the gigantic Sarawak Chamber which is reputed to be the largest*

Above: *Situated between Miri and Bintulu in northern Sarawak, this view of the Great Cave in the Niah National Park ㉗ shows the enormous size of this cavern compared to the outside rainforest trees and the old houses for bird's nest collectors.*

Right: *The Pinnacles, needle-sharp limestone outcrops, are located on the flanks of Gunung Api, a forest-clad limestone peak in the Gunung Mulu National Park.*

in the world, as well as mountainous rainforests and under-ground rivers.

Left: *The bizarre-looking rhinoceros hornbill (Buceros rhinoceros), derives its name from the horn-like casque on its head.*

SABAH

The Land Below the Wind, as Sabah is also known, is situated in the northern corner of Borneo, and is dominated by Mount Kinabalu. At 4101m (13,455ft), it is the highest mountain peak between the Himalayas and New Guinea. Sabah's reputation as a land of adventure is legendary and the mountainous state with its 1440km-long (895-mile) coastline offers not only the famed summit climb of Kinabalu but a wide range of attractions, including Malaysia's best diving, orang-utan sanctuaries and a diverse and colourful populace.

Above: Wooden fishing boats crowd the harbour at Kota Kinabalu,(28) the capital of Sabah, which was built from the ashes of its predecessor, Jesselton, after World War II.

Opposite: The tiled dome of the state mosque towers above the palm trees and a water village on the outskirts of Kota Kinabalu.

Above and right: Dried chillies are displayed in bamboo trays and slices of watermelon tempt passers-by in Kota Kinabalu's Central Market.

Above: *When the dawn light strikes Victoria Peak, Mount Kinabalu's second highest, the surrounding state is still in darkness.*

Below: *The ascent is not technically difficult, but is a gruelling slog even for the very fit.*

Opposite: *Granite outcrops, known as The Donkey's Ears, rear above the stunted forests at the base of the treeline on Mount Kinabalu ① near the overnight rest station, which is a steady climb to about 3353m (11,000ft) above sea level.*

Above: *The vast granite summit plateau is striated by ancient glaciers from a time in the distant past when Borneo was joined to the Malay Peninsula. The mountain pushed through the earth's surface 1.5 million years ago and, according to geologists, is still growing.*

Right: *This mountain stream flows from Mount Kinabalu, the source of many of Sabah's rivers, including the Kinabatangan.*

Opposite and above: *At the Orang-utan Rehabilitation Centre* ㉙ *at Sepilok outside Sandakan on the east coast of Sabah, illegally captured individuals, or those saved from forests during clearing operations, are retrained to help them adjust to normal rainforest life. Orang-utans occur only in the forests of Borneo and Sumatra. In recent years, populations have declined as large areas of forest have been cleared for agriculture and plantations.*

Above: *Of the estimated 2500 species of Bornean orchids, most grow on trees high above the ground. Mount Kinabalu Park* ㉚ *is a favourite viewing area; a huge collection of lowland orchids can be viewed at the agricultural research station in Tenom in Sabah.*

Left: *The Rajah Brooke birdwing butterfly was named after the Brooke family who controlled Sarawak for over a century.*

Above and opposite: *Pulau Sipadan,* ㉛ *situated in the Sulawesi Sea off the southeast coast of Sabah, is Malaysia's only oceanic island. It arose from the ocean floor during a volcanic eruption and, as a result, the island boasts the nation's sheerest and deepest dives. The waters around the island abound with marine life of all descriptions, and the only resort is usually booked out by underwater enthusiasts.*

Above: *At Kota Kinabalu,* ㉘ *passengers board the express ferry en route to Pulau Labuan. Commanding the approaches to Brunei Bay, off the southwest coast of Sabah, the island of Labuan is a federal territory under the control of Kuala Lumpur, and serves as an offshore financial centre and duty-free port.*

Left: *This boy on board his father's boat at Kota Kinabalu is a Bajau ('Sea Gypsy'), and part of a Muslim community which lives by the sea.*

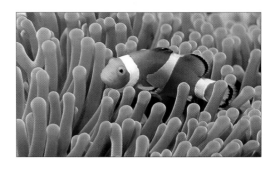

Opposite: *Visibility is often up to 100m (328ft) in the waters around Pulau Sipadan where both the hawksbill turtle (Eretmochelys imbricata), seen here, and green turtle (Chelonia mydas) are sometimes spotted. Both are endangered. The hawksbill's carapace is used for tortoiseshell and the green turtle is hunted for its meat. After lumbering up the sandy beaches of the island where it lays its eggs, the green turtle then returns to the sea. When the eggs hatch, the baby turtles make their way back down the beach and out to sea unassisted, a process fraught with danger from marauding birds and other hungry marine creatures.*

Above: *The harlequin sweetlips (Plectorhinchus chaetodonoides) can be seen in large schools in shallow waters, 'vacuuming' the ocean floor with its broad, fleshy lips in search of molluscs.*

Below left and right: *Brilliant red featherstars enliven the reefs around Pulau Sipadan, where the reef wall drops away to an awe-inspiring depth of 600m (1970ft).*

Above: *The clown anemone fish (Amphiprion ocellaris) lives amongst the tentacles of a large anemone, which provides protection against predators, and is also a source of food.*

Below: *This thorny oyster (Spondylus aurantius) is filtering food particles through its gills.*

Following page: *An attractive chick blind made of split bamboo advertizes local sarong brands in the town of Kuala Terengganu.*

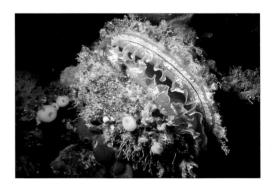

First published in 1996 by
New Holland (Publishers) Ltd
London • Cape Town • Sydney • Singapore

24 Nutford Place
London W1H 6DQ
United Kingdom

80 McKenzie Street
Cape Town 8001
South Africa

3/2 Aquatic Drive
Frenchs Forest, NSW 2086
Australia

ISBN 1 85368 911 4

Writer: Khadijah Moore
Concept designer: Alix Gracie
Publishing manager: Mariëlle Renssen
Editor: Jane Maliepaard
Senior art editor: Trinity Fry
DTP cartographer: John Loubser
Consultant: Ken Scriven

Reproduction by Unifoto (Pty) Ltd
Printed and bound in Singapore by Tien Wah
Press (Pte) Ltd

Photographic acknowledgments

David Bowden: 5 (top left), 9 (bottom right), 13 (top right and bottom left), 16 (top and bottom right), 19 (bottom left), 23 (bottom), 30 (bottom right), 33 (top), 45, 53 (top left), 61 (top) **Gerald Cubitt:** 5 (top right and bottom right), 30 (top), 41, 53 (top right), 53 (bottom right), 61 (bottom), 68 (top right), 72 (bottom, centre and right), 73, 75 (bottom left), back cover (centre right) **Jill Gocher:** front cover (right, top and bottom), 3 (bottom right), 4 (centre and bottom right), 6 (bottom right), 7 (top), 8 (top), 10 (bottom right), 11 (bottom right), 12 (top and bottom, left and right), 13 (top left), 13 (bottom right), 14–15, 20 (top right and bottom, left and right), 25, 27 (bottom right), 33 (bottom right), 40 (top right), 40 (bottom, left and right), 42, 43 (top, left and right), 44 (top and centre, left and right), 46 (top and bottom), 47, 48, 49 (top and bottom, left and right), 50 (top, centre and bottom left), 58 (bottom), 59, 62, 63 (centre), 64 (bottom right), 67 (top), 69, 71 (top and

bottom right), 72 (bottom left), 75 (top and bottom right), back cover (bottom left) **Hutchinson Library:** 66, 72 (top) **Hutchinson Library (John Hatt):** 67 (bottom left) **Hutchinson Library (Juliet Highet):** 4 (top) **Hutchinson Library (Jeremy Horner):** 10 (bottom left), 11 (centre left) **Hutchinson Library (R. Ian Lloyd):** 11 (top), 26, 60 **Hutchinson Library (Christine Pemberton):** 27 (top), 76 (bottom right) **Hutchinson Library (Angela Silvertop):** 6 (top) **Jack Jackson:** 4 (bottom left), 5 (bottom left), 74, 78, 79 (centre left and bottom, left and right) **Patrick Lim:** 19 (top right and bottom right), 23 (top left), 27 (bottom left), 54 (bottom right), 56, 57 (bottom left) **Photo Access (David Steele):** front cover (centre right), 38–39 **Linda Pitkin:** 79 (centre right) **Radin Mohd Noh Saleh:** 1, 2 (bottom), 3 (top and bottom left), 9 (top and bottom left), 11 (bottom left), 20 (top left), 30 (bottom left), 37 (top), 40 (top left), 40 (centre), 44 (bottom left),

57 (centre right), 80, back cover (bottom right) **Struik Image Library (Andrew Bannister):** front cover (main photographic, inset and bird motif), 2 (top), 6 (bottom left), 7 (bottom), 8 (left), 10 (top), 16 (bottom left), 17, 18, 19 (top left), 21, 22, 23 (top right), 24 (top and bottom, left and right), 28 (top, left and right, and bottom), 29, 30 (bottom centre), 31, 32, 33 (bottom, left and centre), 34 (top and bottom), 35, 36, 37 (centre and bottom), 43 (centre and bottom, left and right), 44 (bottom right), 50 (bottom right), 51, 52, 53 (centre, left and right), 54 (top and bottom left), 55, 57 (top left and centre left), 57 (bottom, centre and right), 58 (top and centre), 63 (top and bottom, left and right), 64 (top, centre, left and right, and bottom left), 65, 67 (bottom right), 68 (top left and bottom, left and right), 70, 71 (bottom left), 76 (top and bottom left), back cover (top left and top right) **Lawson Wood:** 77, 79 (top right), back cover (centre left).